THE BRITISH SOLDIER IN THE 20TH CENTURY

Written and illustrated by

MIKE CHAPPELL

WESSEX MILITARY PUBLISHING

Published in 1988 by
Wessex Military Publishing
1A High Street
Hatherleigh, Devon EX20 3JH
© Copyright 1988 Wessex
Military Publishing

ISBN 1 870498 04 6

Typeset and printed in Great Britain by
Toptown Printers Limited
Vicarage Lawn, Barnstaple, North Devon
England

Photographic processing by CJP Photographic
2 North Street, Okehampton, Devon

Right: "Battledress, serge" – the original pattern of 1939. Note the button and tab arrangement for drawing together the trousers at the ankle. (Courtesy Bill Reynolds)

Below: In 1939 and 1940, Service Dress was worn alongside Battledress until sufficient stocks of B.D. became available; a case demonstrated by these three junior N.C.O.s of the Royal Engineers. (Courtesy Anne Chappell)

Rear Cover: Her Majesty the Queen inspecting a Guard of Honour from the 5th Glosters in the mid-1960s. The Territorial Army continued to be issued with Battledress after it had ceased to be worn by the Regular Army. (Author's collection)

5 : Battledress 1939-1960

Battledress had replaced Service Dress as the field uniform of the British Army by 1940. Like Service Dress, the new uniform started life as a loose-fitting, practical garment, and was "smartened-up" in later patterns – thereby losing much of its original suitability as a dress for battle. It was gradually replaced by Combat Dress in the 1950s and 1960s.

Large stocks of clothing and equipment were held in British Ordnance stores at the end of the Great War of 1914-18; enough to meet the needs of Britain's small peacetime army for many years. Research and development aimed at improving field uniforms was carried out in the 1930s, but on a very small scale, geared mainly to the needs of "mechanisation" (as the change from animal to mechanical transport was called). A field uniform in drab serge, remarkably similar to Australian service dress, appeared and underwent troop trials. Following these, the experimental uniform was made up in denim along with an even newer design of field uniform in the same material. (The newer uniform was modelled on the skiing clothing then fashionable and consisted of a short jacket – termed a blouse – and very baggy trousers gathered at the ankles.) Both forms of dress were shown to the press in 1938, and the photographs taken on that occasion clearly show the "ski suit" to be the uniform that eventually developed into Battledress. (B.D.)

Uniforms made from denim were quickly seen to be too flimsy for protection from the north-western European climate. (A fact that may astonish the generations of British soldiers ordered out into winter weather in "Overalls, denim".) The "ski suit" uniform was therefore made up in Service Dress drab serge and christened "Battledress, serge". Manufacture in quantity began in 1939, the first recipients of the new uniform being the National Service "militiamen" called up in the early summer of that year.

Following Britain's declaration of war in September 1939 both Service

The late King George VI inspecting a formation in Scotland, 1943. Note the unfaced collars of the Battledress, serge of the officers at centre. The wartime censor has obliterated all sensitive insignia. (Author's collection)

Dress and Battledress were worn on active service until sufficient stocks of the latter became available. This had been achieved by the spring of 1940, and from then on Battledress became the temperate climate field uniform of the British Army for the next two decades. Over that period British factories produced five patterns of Battledress which were worn by British troops, with American factories supplying a sixth. Battledress was also made in Canada and other Commonwealth countries. These patterns, distinctly different from British and American B.D., were also worn by British soldiers – the Canadian pattern in

particular. The many patterns of Battledress each underwent modification, both official and unofficial, and these make the study of this uniform complicated but absorbing. The following text describes all the patterns worn by the British Army.

Battledress, Serge

(The original pattern. Sometimes called "1937-pattern".)

No sooner had the first issues of this pattern been made than the uniform's shortcomings became obvious to it's wearers. Some were design faults and others were due to the poor manufacturing and inspection standards of some factories.

(The author has a B.D. blouse, bearing an inspector's stamp, but cut and put together in an unbelievably crude manner when compared to post-war manufacturing standards.) Instructions were issued to ensure that certain seams were double-sewn and buttons more securely attached. Further regulations altered the position of pockets and reduced the generosity of the cut to comply with wartime economy standards. Collars were lined with drill to reduce rashes on sensitive necks, and trousers were lined with shirt material in the region of the lower back for added protection.

Officers were originally permitted to have their suits of B.D. made up by military tailors. These were made in a variety of materials, styles and fit, but the practice was soon abolished, due to wartime economies, and all officers were ordered to wear issue patterns of B.D. Apart from their badges of rank, the distinguishing mark of an officer in Battledress was his open collar, collar-attached shirt and neck-tie. (This privilege was extended to off-duty Other Ranks towards the end of World War Two, following much discontent at a time when the neckties of U.S. soldiers put the British in the position of poor relations.)

Officers', Warrant Officers' and N.C.O.s' badges of rank authorised for wear on B.D. were those previously worn on Service Dress, except that metal badges were supposed to be replaced by cloth embroidered patterns. This regulation was frequently ignored. Regimental and Corps titles were limited to cloth slip-on titles, showing designation in black embroidery on drab; but from 1939 onwards colourful distinctions to indicate Regiment, Corps, Formation and branch of service began to appear, at first unofficially and then with official sanction. By 1941 most soldiers in Battledress were wearing a highly-coloured array of insignia on the sleeves and shoulders of their uniform, a display that continued throughout the life of B.D. (Off-duty, in barracks and sometimes on active service coloured Regimental "field-service" caps were extensively worn with this uniform in World War Two.)

Troops of the 154 Infantry Brigade, 51st (Highland) Division after the battle at Franleu, France, June 1940 in which the 7th Argyll and Sutherland Highlanders sustained over 500 casualties. Two men wear Battledress, serge. (IWM photo)

A pattern of Greatcoat similar to that worn by officers was introduced with B.D., replacing the two patterns formerly worn. All greatcoats now had pleated backs, held in by a half-belt. The intention was that the belt could be undone to allow the greatcoat to be worn *over* equipment – a practice hardly ever seen. Raincoats were still the privilege of officers. Other ranks were expected to use their groundsheets to keep off the rain. Puttees were rarely worn with the new uniform, webbing anklets being the prescribed item. (These were widely referred to as "gaiters".) Black leather ammunition boots, of the pattern previously issued, were worn with B.D., but some officers were permitted to continue to wear brown leather boots according to Regimental custom and practice.

When worn with woollen underwear, shirts, pullovers, etc. Battledress provided good protection in cold weather and, perhaps, better protection in the wet than some more recent designs. There is evidence that American troops, equipped with the cotton-fabric combat dress, obtained and wore British Battledress. British factories turned out a Battledress to U.S. Army design for American soldiers in 1944/45.

Overalls, Denim

(Invariably called simply, "denims")

Introduced into service at the same time as B.D., "denims" replaced the old "canvas" overalls as the work or fatigue uniform of the British Army. Made to be put on *over* B.D., denims looked ridiculous if worn on their own, hanging shapelessly and looking distinctly unmilitary. A "fit" could only be obtained by wearing denims several sizes too small. (This usually meant that trouser legs and sleeves were too short.) There were several patterns of denims, the first being an exact copy of the serge B.D. Later patterns had removeable buttons to facilitate laundering, plain, unpleated pockets and trousers without belt loops.

Towards the end of World War Two denim Battledress was worn extensively on active service, particularly in Italy, where it was worn in lieu of khaki drill, and in Northwest Europe, where it was worn over B.D. for added protection from the cold. Denims were also much utilised by the crews of armoured fighting vehicles until special tank crew uniforms were devised and issued.

The two photographs on this page show a sub-unit of a Light Anti-Aircraft Regt in the U.K., 1941 (above) and on active service in North Africa, 1942. The dress in both photos is Battledress, serge. The contrast shows clearly how it was worn in barracks and "in the field". (Courtesy Bill Reynolds)

Battledress, Serge, 1940 pattern

(Sometimes called the "utility" pattern.)

Devised in 1940, this pattern of B.D. did not begin to be issued until 1942. 1st Army troops photographed in North Africa in late 1942/early 1943 were the first wearers of the 1940 pattern B.D. in action. Economy was the prime consideration for the designers of the 1940 pattern, economy of material and manufacturing effort. The "fly" fastening of the blouse, pockets and cuffs were replaced with exposed buttons, the brass buttons on the original pattern were replaced by plastic buttons, trouser belt and trouser cuff loops were dispensed with, as was one of the inside breast pockets. The fullness of the blouse was further reduced, giving the 1940 pattern B.D. a distinctive "snug" appearance.

Rifle Regiments took advantage of the introduction of the 1940 pattern blouse by replacing its buttons with their traditional "black buttons". Some officers also reverted to a fashion of the previous war by wearing leather buttons.

Photographs show that, throughout the life of Battledress, blouses and trousers of contrasting patterns were frequently issued and worn, either for economy or in an attempt to match the varying shades of cloth to avoid what was termed the "sports jacket and flannels" effect.

Battledress, Olive Drab, W.A.

("American" B.D. – the W.A. stood for War Aid.)

The grand scheme of production of war material called for British clothing factories to make U.S. uniforms for American soldiers in Europe, whilst at the same time American factories were producing Battledress for British soldiers. This pattern of B.D. was manufactured in the United States from about 1943 onwards and shipped, apparently, to the Middle East for issue to British forces, Commonwealth troops and Greek, Albanian, Yugoslav and Italian partisans. Most photographs of American B.D. being worn by British personnel show it in this theatre. Troops seen wearing it in the U.K. and North-west Europe had

Above: **Gunner J.J. Doherty of the 25/9th (Londonderry) H.A.A. Regt, Royal Artillery, Italy 1943. Note the "R.A." titles and Arm-of-Service strips on his 1940 pattern B.D. – shown, badged for 1945, at right. Note the four good conduct chevrons, five war service chevrons, despatch rider's badge, Anti-Aircraft Command formation sign and ribbons for war service in Africa and Italy. (Courtesy Richard Doherty)**

obviously been issued with it in Italy or Egypt before returning to the U.K.

The main recognition feature of American B.D. was that the blouse "fly" front was retained, but that the pockets and cuffs had exposed buttons. Also the trousers retained the belt loops of the British first pattern. Veterans have also confirmed to the author the superiority of material and manufacture of American B.D. Examination of surviving items would seem to point this up. It was clearly a sought-after uniform; many senior British officers being photographed wearing it.

Battledress, Serge. Canadian pattern

Another much sought-after pattern of B.D. was that manufactured in

Canada. Made in the style of the "original" British pattern, Canadian Battledress was superior in materials and manufacture. Its colour was a distinctive bronze-green, quite different from the drab (nearly always referred to as "khaki") shade of British uniform. During World War Two Canadian B.D. was frequently worn by British soldiers whenever they could "acquire" it. After the war the stocks of Canadian B.D. held in British Ordnance stores were issued to British units after the withdrawal of the Canadian Army from the Middle East and North-west Europe. In the late 1940s it was quite common to see British soldiers in the Canadian uniform.

(continued on page 18)

Battledress, Serge

The main figure depicts Brigadier Manley James, V.C., M.C. when in command of 128 (Hampshire) Infantry Brigade, 46th Infantry Division, Tunisia 1943. Brigadier James wears the uniform typical of an officer of his rank at this period. His "Battledress, Serge" is the original, unmodified pattern, identified by the unlined collar and plain field dressing pocket. Note the Service Dress cap, badges of rank and gorget patches of a Brigadier. The latter is shown in detail below, with a General officer's gorget patch on the right. Both replaced the scarlet cord boss (shown in detail) worn with Battledress in 1940/41. Below the Divisional sign on his sleeve, the Brigadier wears the Staff arm-of-service strip. A-O-S strips were worn on B.D. from 1940. Shown below are those for the Royal Armoured Corps (top left), Royal Artillery (top right), Royal Electrical and Mechanical Engineers (bottom left) and the Reconnaissance Corps (bottom right). Shown in detail also are the first pattern blouse buckle, brass buttons and collar hooks from Battledress, Serge, along with a shoulder title for the Rifle Brigade and a button and split ring attachment for denim overalls.

The photograph at left shows Major-General Sir Percy Hobart when in command of the 11th Armoured Division, c.1942. Note Sir Percy's black beret and faced collar to his Battledress, Serge. The lower photo shows the label sewn to the inner pocket of a Battledress, Serge blouse. (Author's collection)

At the centre of the colour plate a Corporal of a Motor Battalion of the Rifle Brigade wears the Other Rank pattern greatcoat. Note the Regimental black buttons, chevrons and Rifles' A-O-S strip (the only insignia supposed to have been worn on this garment, other than badges of rank). At this time the khaki beret was the exclusive preserve of the motor battalions and units of the Reconnaissance Corps. Our subject is painted from photos taken in Italy in 1944.

Also photographed in Italy was Fusilier Frank Jefferson, 2nd Lancashire Fusiliers, 11 Infantry Brigade, 78th Infantry Division. Fusilier Jefferson destroyed a German self-propelled gun and "saw-off" a second in an act of bravery that eventually earned him the Victoria Cross. Not the least part of Jefferson's effort was to fire his PIAT (Projector, Infantry, Anti-Tank – a spigot mortar) from the hip. In doing so he risked injury from the weapon and death from the projectile. Fusilier Jefferson was portrayed with his PIAT and in denim overalls, the standard British combat wear in the hot months in Italy at that time.

Insignia in the 78th Division was limited to the Divisional sign and a Regimental "flash". These were worn on Battledress and on "slides" for wear on shirt or denim blouse epaulettes.

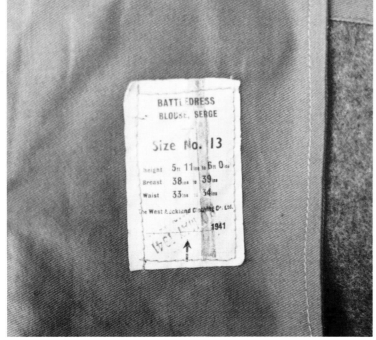

COLOUR PLATE B

1940 pattern and American Battledress

*In 1944 the Reconnaissance Corps dis-
carded their khaki berets in favour of the
Royal Armoured Corps' black headgear. The
figure at left shows a Recce Corps Captain
just before this event. The 43rd Reconnaissance were the Recce unit for the 43rd
(Wessex) Infantry Division, having been the
5th Glosters before conversion.*

*Our subject wears the standard 1940
pattern Battledress with officer's webbing.
He is armed with a No. 2 Enfield revolver
and a Mk III Sten machine carbine. Note the
Arm-of-Service backing colour to his stars
("pips"), Divisional sign and Corps title.
(All shown in detail below.) Not shown in
detail are the Recce Arm-of-Service strip, the
wound stripe on the left cuff and the ribbon
of what then was known as the "1939-43
Star". Note also the button detail compared
to that for American B.D.*

*At right is shown a Sergeant of Special Air
Service, Italy, 1945. Our subject is extensively clothed and armed by Lease-lend
(Lend-lease?), wearing "Battle Dress, (the
Americans used two words) Olive Drab, War
Aid", a U.S. Army O.D. shirt and carrying
an American MIAI .30 calibre carbine in
addition to his pistol. Note the sand-hued
beret, S.A.S. wings worn on the left breast to
denote an active service parachute descent,
and the ribbons of the Military Medal and
Africa Star. The wings are shown in detail
below as is the S.A.S. title worn on battledress at times.*

*The British authorities, inspired no doubt
by their American counterparts, started to
issue campaign ribbons before the end of the
war. The first two to appear were the 1939-
1943 Star (later called the 1939-1945 Star
and issued to virtually everyone who saw
combat) and the Africa Star. Issues began in
early 1944. The 1939-43 Stars going mostly
to veterans of the campaign in France in
1939 and 1940, and the Africa Star being
awarded to the men of the victorious 8th and
1st Armies. These were distinguished by a
small silver '8' or '1' worn on the central part
of the ribbon.*

*Shown at right are front and back views
of the American Battledress, with represen-
tative examples of the labels sewn into the
garments. (The photographs are courtesy of
Mr Dean L. Kleffman of Pekin, Illinois,
U.S.A. Mr Kleffman is a collector of British
Battledress who has generously supplied
much information to the author.)*

*N.B. Reproduction of uniform labels is
included as an aid to collectors. With the
scarcity of the earlier patterns of Battledress, their value has risen in a quite
remarkable manner. "Counterfeiting" of
Service Dress is already happening. A know-
ledge of markings should enable collectors to
avoid bogus items of Battledress.*

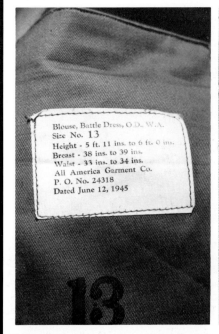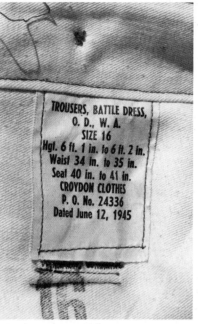

11

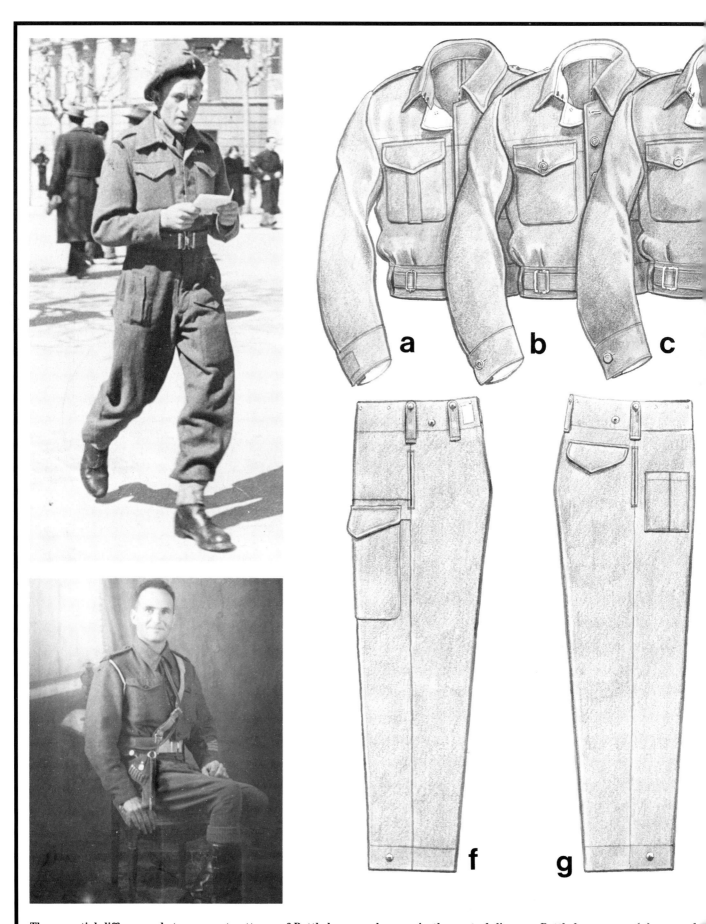

The essential differences between most patterns of Battledress can be seen in the central diagram. Battledress, serge (a); conceal[ed] buttons and pleated pockets. Battledress, 1940 pattern (b); exposed buttons – no pocket pleats. Battledress, O.D., W.A. (American) (c) like original pattern but no pocket pleats and exposed buttons on pockets and cuffs. Battledress, 1946 pattern (d); 1940 pattern wi[th] fly front, pleated pockets and faced collar. Battledress, 1947 pattern (e); 1946 pattern with pleated cuffs and "American" collar. Th[e] Battledress, serge trousers are shown at (f) and (g). American trousers were similar, but had exposed buttons on pocket flaps; as d[id] the 1940 pattern, which had no belt loops or cuff tabs. 1949 pattern B.D. trousers, (h) and (i), had 3 belt loops and a different pock[et] arrangement.

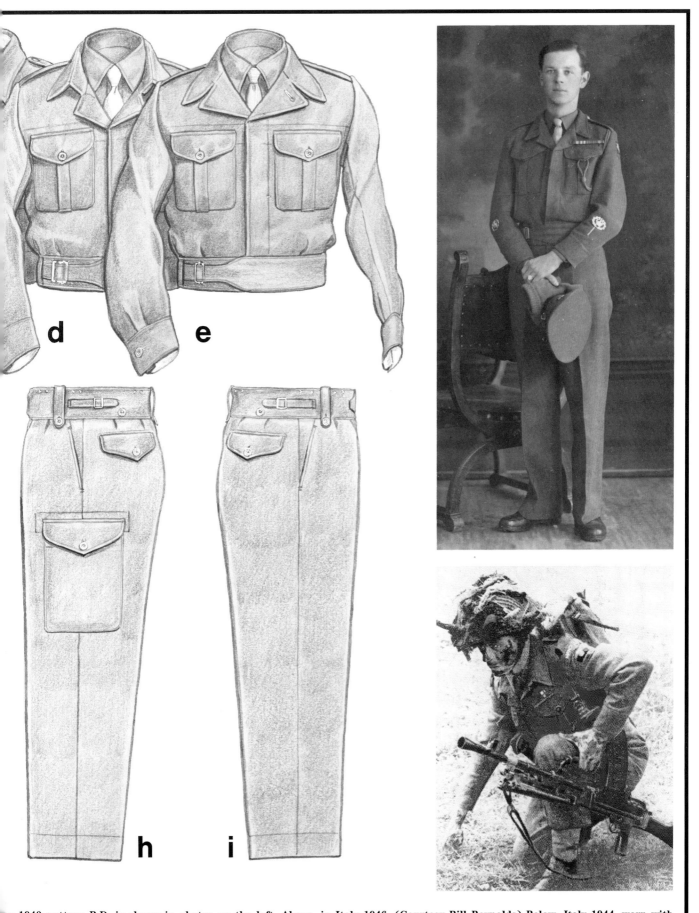

d   e

h   i

e 1940 pattern B.D. is shown in photos on the left. Above, in Italy 1946. (Courtesy Bill Reynolds) Below, Italy 1944, worn with
Don-R's" breeches and boots. (Courtesy Richard Doherty) The photo at top right shows a "tailored" Battledress, serge worn by W.O.II
(MS) A.J. Moore, King's Regiment, in Klagenfurt, 1946. (Courtesy Tony Moore) Below this a private of the Manchesters wears the 1946
ttern B.D., 1948. (Author's collection)

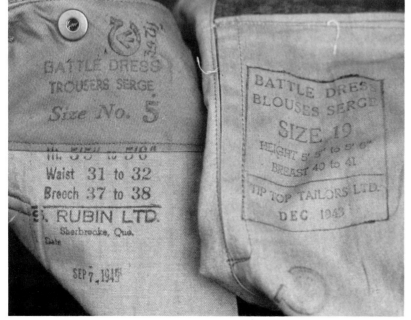

Battledress, 1945 to 1949

When the Canadian Army withdrew from Europe in 1945 and 1946, they left behind the stocks of their clothing being held by British Ordnance. This was subsequently issued to British units. The Quartermaster of the 1st Royal Irish Fusiliers (Austria, 1946) was one of those who secured Canadian Battledress for the men of his battalion performing guards and ceremonial. Photographs of the 1st R.I.F. at this time show a very high standard of "turnout", as depicted by the central figure.

Note the bronze/green colour of the Fusilier's Canadian Battledress when compared to British drab ("khaki"). Skilfull tailoring and much use of an iron could turn a shapeless B.D. into an elegant outfit, especially when it had to pass the inspection of a "keen" Adjutant. Note the Divisional sign, the shamrock of the 38th (Irish) Infantry Brigade with the R.I.F. triangle picked out in white, Signaller's badge, Good conduct chevron and ribbons of the Italian campaign. The Fusilier's weapon is the No. 4 rifle and bayonet. Shown in detail are the blouse buckle and metal button common to all Canadian B.D.

Late-war manufactured Canadian B.D. had the collar hooks replaced by a tab. This was copied in the British 1946 pattern blouse shown at left, being worn by a trooper of the Lothian and Border Horse in 1948. Note the serge "facings" and details of the collar, shoulder title and Divisional sign of the 52nd (Lowland) Division T.A. Medal ribbons are for service in N. Africa, Italy, etc. and the Territorial Efficiency Medal.

The figure at bottom right is of a Sergeant-pilot of the Glider Pilot Regiment in 1950. Our subject wears the 1947 pattern B.D. blouse with the "American" collar open. The detail illustration below shows it closed. Note the newly-introduced badge of the Glider Pilot Regiment, Regimental title, Airborne Forces formation sign, pilot's wings and medal ribbons for service in North-west Europe and Palestine. Shown in detail are the wings worn by 2nd Glider pilots from 1944 to 1951. Members of the Regiment continued to fly light aircraft for the Army long after gliders became obsolete. Eventually they were absorbed into the Army Air Corps in the late 1950s.

The first neck-ties issued to British Other ranks were shabby, cotton items of a pale khaki shade. The soldiers responded by buying the superior woven ties favoured by officers. This led to further expenditure of wrath on the part of authority until they bowed to the inevitable and arranged for "knitted" ties to be issued.

The photographs at left show front and rear views of Canadian B.D., with details of typical marking. (Courtesy Mr. Dean L. Kleffman)

Plate C

LOTHIAN & BORDER HORSE

COLOUR PLATE D

The 1949 pattern Battledress

The last real war in which British troops wore Battledress was the Korean War of 1950-1953. (Battledress continued to be worn in many later conflicts which successive British Governments shrank from calling wars.)

The 29th Independant Brigade Group arrived in Korea from the U.K. in late 1950, with nothing but Battledress and windproof suits to fend off the worst of the Korean Winter. With the 29th were the men of the 1st Glosters, soon to win fame for their stand on the Imjin River in April 1951. The main figure depicts a Vickers Machine Gun "No. 1" of Support Company, 1 Glosters at the time of the battle. He wears the 1949 pattern Battledress and a heavy duty pullover and carries the Vickers tripod, dial sight, aiming post and cleaning rod. His '44 pattern equipment comprises of No. 2 pistol, case, ammunition case and compass. Note his two cap badges, Regimental title, Wessex Brigade "flash", badge of appointment and machine gun qualification badge. His ribbons mark him as a veteran of World War Two — as were many of the reservists who packed the ranks of 29 Bde. On his right shoulder he wears the formation sign of the 29th Brigade, shown in detail below.

At left, a Colour Sergeant of the Grenadier Guards shows the 1949 pattern B.D. as worn in its "smartened-up" version in the 1950s — well-pressed and tailored to a snug fit. Note his cap, titles and special badges of rank.

Regimental titles worn on Battledress post-war are a study in themselves. Shown on this plate are those of the Border Regiment (commemorating service as airlanding troops) and the amalgamated North Somerset Yeomanry and 44th Royal Tanks (both Territorial Army). Few Cavalry regiments ever wore cloth titles on Battledress, but chose to wear the metal titles previously worn with Service Dress. (11th Hussars shown here.)

In hot weather, Battledress "shirtsleeve order" was often adopted for comfort — for work, training and in action. The tradition of the British soldier taking off his jacket and rolling up his sleeves is a long and honourable one! Below left is a Corporal of one of the Parachute Battalions in North Africa in 1943. Note his collarless shirt (shown in detail in the photo at bottom right of recruits at the Border Regiment Depot in the late 1930s), Airborne pattern B.D. trousers and Fairbairn-Sykes knife.

The British Army began to issue shirts with collars at the time they authorised the wearing of ties. (Many American Army shirts were obtained from the U.S. under Lease-lend at this time.) Eventually the "shirt, khaki flannel" appeared in the late 1940s. It is being worn in the photo top right. (Depot Glosters, 1955.)

17

Battledress, 1946 pattern

In 1946 a new pattern of B.D. blouse was authorised. It featured a "faced" collar which could either be worn closed, by means of a tab, or open with a tie. The fly front opening and pleated pockets of the "original" pattern B.D. were re-introduced. The 1946 pattern B.D. blouse was introduced at a time when the other ranks of the British Army were only permitted to wear ties when "off-duty" or "walking out" and had to wear their Battledress fastened at the neck at other times.

Battledress, 1947 pattern

A year after the introduction of the 1946 pattern B.D., yet another design of blouse was authorised featuring a dual-purpose collar. This time the collar of the American "Ike" jacket was copied and incorporated into what was termed the 1947-pattern B.D. Sleeves of a more generous cut were introduced with this blouse.

Battledress, 1949 pattern

The final pattern of British Battledress appeared after the decision had been taken that ties would be worn by all ranks at all times. The blouse was similar to the 1947 pattern but had a smaller, stepped, collar. The trousers, however, were entirely different from previous patterns and featured belt loops, waist tabs, slanted pockets, two hip pockets and a side-mounted map pocket.

The 1949 pattern B.D. remained the standard, temperate climate field uniform of the British Army until fully replaced by Combat Dress, which had first been issued in Korea but did not become generally available until the late 1950s.

Battledress as a field uniform

Woollen serge, as a material for a field uniform, was seen to be obsolete when the United States Army introduced their "layered" concept of combat clothing in 1943. The British followed the lead of the Americans, introducing their own Combat Dress as a winter uniform during the Korean War. It may be said, therefore, that the useful life of Battledress was just over ten years.

(continued on page 24)

Above: **Gunner, Royal Artillery, Italy 1944, showing the tie being worn with the 1940 pattern B.D. blouse. (Courtesy Bill Reynolds)** *Below:* **signallers of the 6th Royal West Kents, 78th Infantry Division, at Cassino – March 1944. They man a "Wireless Set No. 18" and wear American B.D. (Author's collection)**

Above: **The Royal Tank Regiment crew of a Churchill A.F.V., England 1942. All wear "Overalls, denim". The man on the right has his trousers gathered at the ankle by tabs in lieu of anklets. (Author's collection)** *Below:* **Egypt 1953. A 3.5 inch rocket launcher team of the 1st Border Regiment. Denim overalls became an infantry combat dress in milder climates of the Middle East. (Regimental Museum, the Border Regiment)**

Three photographs of Battledress being worn in action, Normandy 1944. *Above:* **A 6-pounder anti-tank gun crew.** *Left, above:* **A junior officer and Corporal lead their platoon through the ruins of a town.** *Left, below:* **A Corporal directs the fire of his section in a hedgerow fire-fight. The wartime censor has obliterated most insignia. (R.A.O.C. Photographs)**

Above, left: **Men of the 7th Cameronians at annual camp, Devon, late 1940s. Note the "trews". Many men wear Canadian blouses. (Regimental Museum, the Cameronians)**

Below, left: **6/7th Cameronians in the 1950s. All wear the 1949 pattern B.D. (Regimental Museum, the Cameronians)**

Above: **The 5th Bn the King's Regiment at a ceremonial occasion in 1965. 1949 pattern B.D. (Courtesy Tony Moore)**

Right: **Major A.J. Moore T.D., 5th King's, twenty years after the photo on the centre pages was taken. 1949 pattern B.D. (Courtesy Tony Moore)**

Recent experience, however, may have pointed up the ineffectiveness of cotton-based field uniforms in cold/wet climates. Wool protected the British Army in the field in the two world wars of this century, and a return to that material may well be overdue. The biggest criticism levied against Battledress was the design of the blouse. Had the Australian-type field uniform of the early 1930s been adopted much of this criticism would have been avoided.

Whatever its shortcomings, Battledress was extensively copied during and after World War Two, by enemy and ally. Germany, the United States, France, Belgium, Holland, Denmark, Australia, New Zealand and South Africa all produced a form of Battledress for field or parade purposes.

Battledress as a parade uniform

The original aim of the designers of Battledress was to provide a comfortable, loose-fitting field uniform, under which more or less layers of clothing could be worn according to the extremes of weather. The comfort of the soldier was uppermost in the minds of the designers and the appearance of the new uniform was not a major consideration. At the time of its introduction it was thought that troops would wear Battledress on active service only, Service Dress being retained for use in barracks, rear areas, etc.

When Battledress became the *only* uniform issued to troops, on a scale of two suits per man, the practice of retaining one suit for "best" became universal. "Best B.D." was tailored to a smart, generally constricting, fit and adorned with much colourful insignia. It was altered, shaved, pressed and stitched into shapes and fashions which left it far removed in appearance from the shapeless "ski suit" of 1938.

As might be expected, the Guards started the practice of having the fullness of the blouse taken in to produce a tight fit that looked smart when on parade. Other regiments copied this fashion. Another sartorial deviation followed the granting of permission to wear ties. This meant that the collar was opened to expose the khaki drill "facing" within. This was at first sponged as it became grubby; then scrubbed; then bleached; and finally replaced with a more durable or more presentable material.

Yet another practice aimed at "smartness" was the practice of wearing "weights". These held the trousers down over the anklets avoiding the concertina effect of the recruit.

Fancy tailoring, blancoed chevrons, Windsor tie-knots, weights (and the "elastics" which followed them), collar facings and fancily pressed creases and pleats were nearly always resisted with great ferocity by NCOs and Warrant Officers bent on stamping out what they saw as anarchy in the matter of dress discipline. Most NCOs considered that Battledress should be worn "as issued". The private soldier – neither wishing to be mistaken for a recruit or seriously reducing his chances at a dance – resisted such regimentation and strove to express his individuality. Deprived of the right to wear civvies, he did the best he could with Battledress, sometimes achieving a quite remarkable result.

The regimental distinctions that are such a feature of British uniform were to have been suppressed on the introduction of Battledress. Highlanders were made to wear trousers like everybody else (as a protection against blister gases) and the brightly coloured caps, overalls, trews, etc. of former times disappeared also. But only for a while. In 1945, with victory secure, most of the distinctions that had been worn with Service Dress were restored for wear with Battledress – at least for parade and ceremonial purposes.

With the abolition of National Service the new British Regular Army adopted a form of Service Dress (No. 2 Dress) for parade wear and Combat Dress for the field. Shortly afterwards the Territorials followed suit to allow Battledress to pass into history.

It is as a uniform of former times that it is now remembered. Those times span the years of defeat and victory in the World War of 1939 to 1945, and the so-called Cold War that followed. To the millions of men who wore the Army "khaki" Battledress during those times, I respectfully dedicate this account.

This booklet is dedicated to the Hatherleigh, Devon, branch of the Royal British Legion; several members of which have provided photographs for publication. The author is most grateful for their generosity and comradeship.